Copyright © 2024 Susana Londono. All rights reserved.

No part of this book, except those portions already in the public domain, may be reproduced in any form or by any electronic or mechanical means without written permission from the author.

All writing, editing and design by Susana Londono.
All images generated with the assistance of ChatGPT.

Toe-tally Funny: Jokes To Make Podiatrists Smile

By: Susana Londono, DPM

This book was made by adding images generated with AI's assistance to a collection of jokes I've thought of or heard. As such, some images are as absurd and surreal as the jokes they accompany, if not more so. I hope these images add another level of enjoyment to make this book even better than the jokes alone.

While largely an exercise in examining AI's limits, this book is also an opportunity for me to share some humor with my fellow podiatrists. Some jokes will make you groan more than they make you laugh, but hopefully you'll appreciate this book as a whole and walk away with a smile (and maybe a few jokes to share with colleagues or patients).

Where does a podiatrist grow vegetables?

In a plantar.

Why did the hippie go to the podiatrist?

He was always trippin'.

Which Star Wars character is a favorite among podiatrists?

Han Sole-o.

Why is it so difficult to read
a podiatrist's research paper?

It's all footnotes.

How did the patient get hallux rigidus?

He stepped on some Viagra.

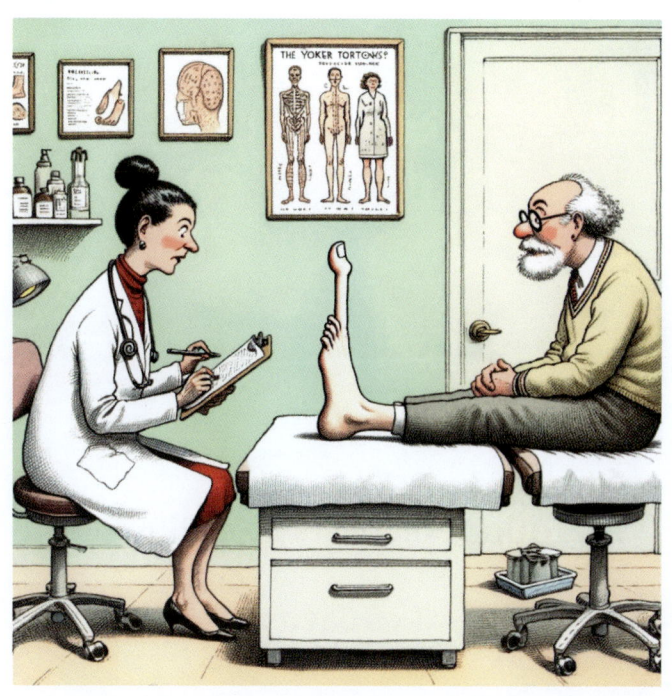

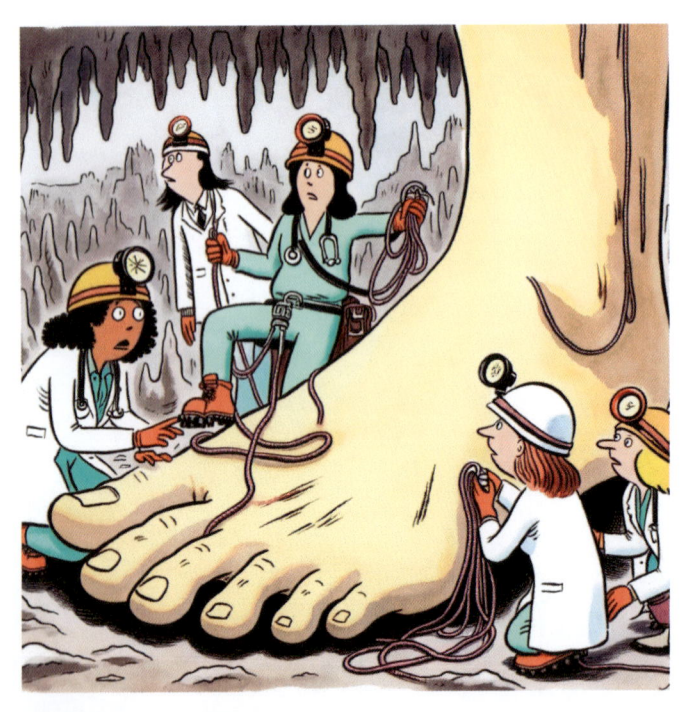

Where do podiatrists go spelunking?

Pes cavus.

Do feet like Nathan?

Yes, they pronate.

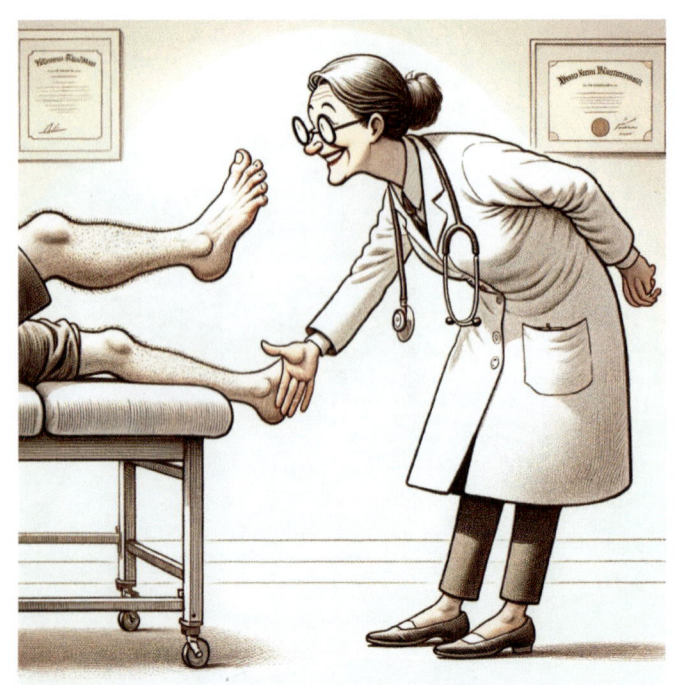

Why did the podiatrist like meeting new patients?

Because they always put their best foot forward.

What's one way a podiatrist
can save your life?

If your shoes are killing you.

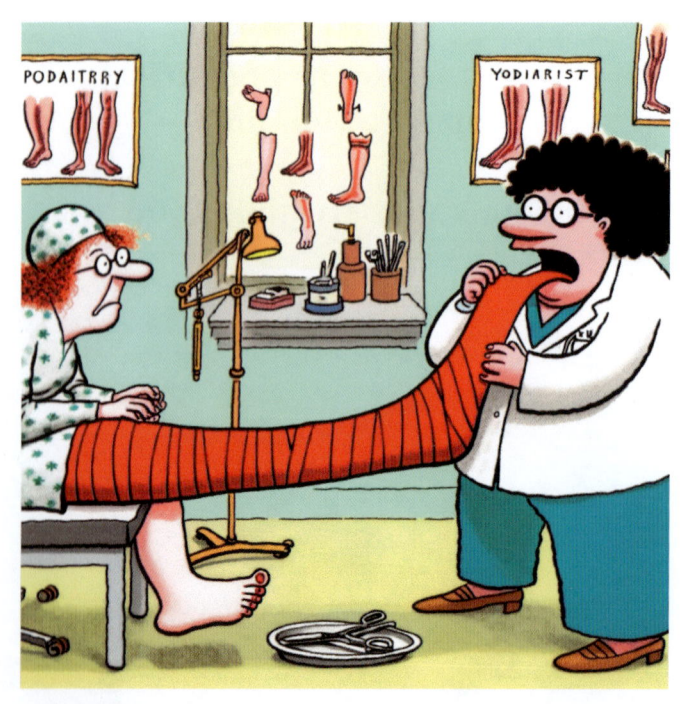

What is a podiatrist's favorite snack?

Fruit by the foot.

Why is a shoe like a French kiss?

There's some tongue.

What is a podiatrist's favorite American folk hero?

Paul Bunion.

How did the podiatrist casually introduce Elizabeth and Francis?

"Liz, Frank."

What's a podiatrist's favorite flying dinosaur called?

Polydactyl.

Why has a podiatrist never climbed Mt. Everest?

They always get distracted by the foothills.

A podiatrist is talking to her
patient and says,

"You have Dutch wooden shoes in your blood."

"Is that bad?"

"Yes, your arteries are clogged."

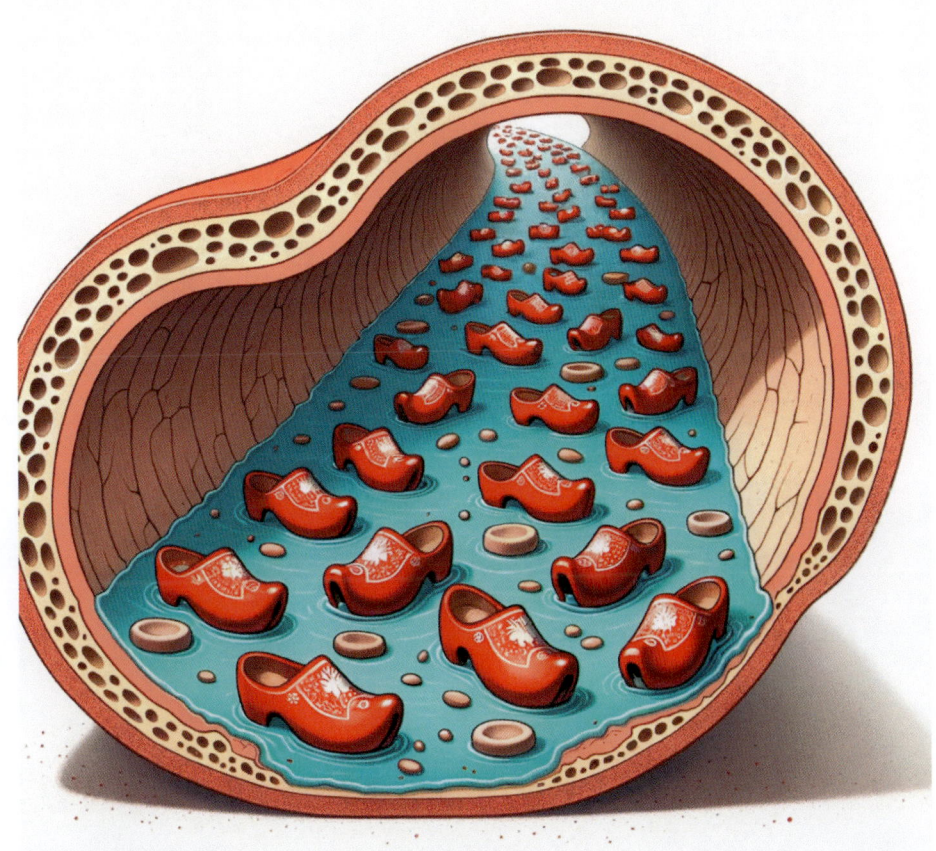

What type of sandwich
do podiatrists order?

A footlong.

How does a podiatrist hang a picture?

With a hammertoe and toenail.

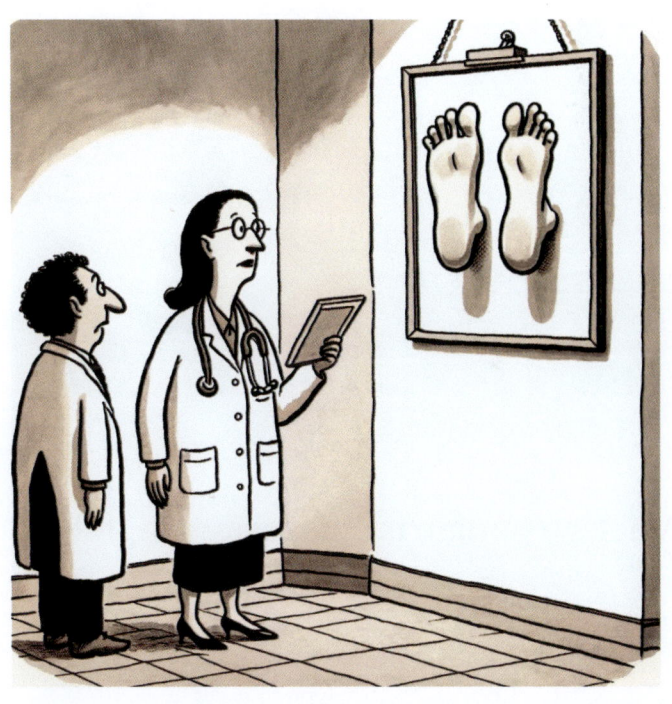

What's a podiatrist's favorite amphibian?

Toed.

Did you hear about the podiatrist who measured every part of a patient's body?

They wanted to take care of everything that was a foot.

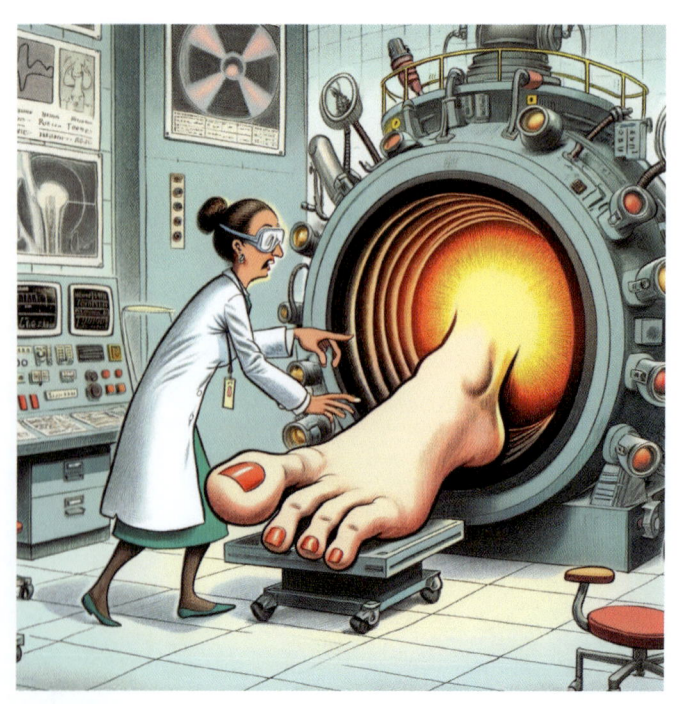

Why did the podiatrist become
a nuclear physicist?

They were already good at fusions.

What does the podiatrist use to heat their grill?

Charcot.

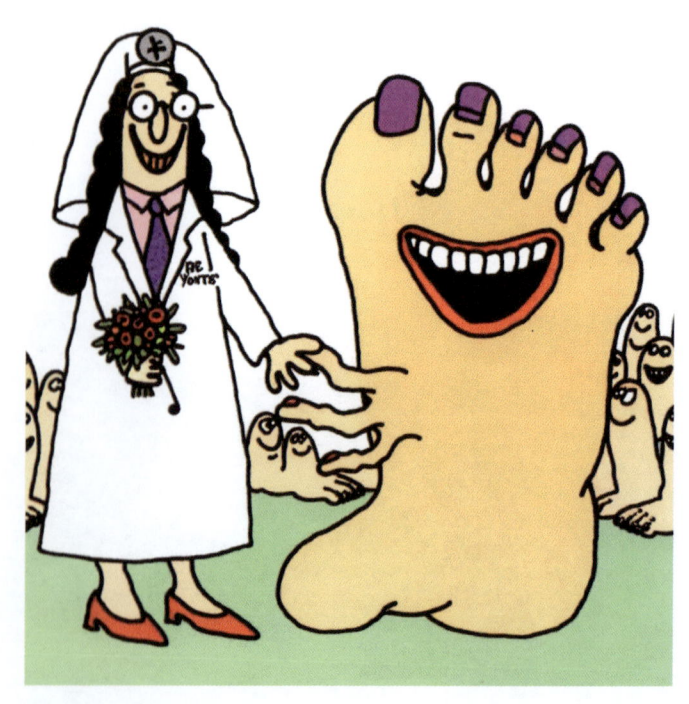

Who did the wounded foot marry?

Debride

Why was the bottom of the foot so strict?

It was a fascia-ist.

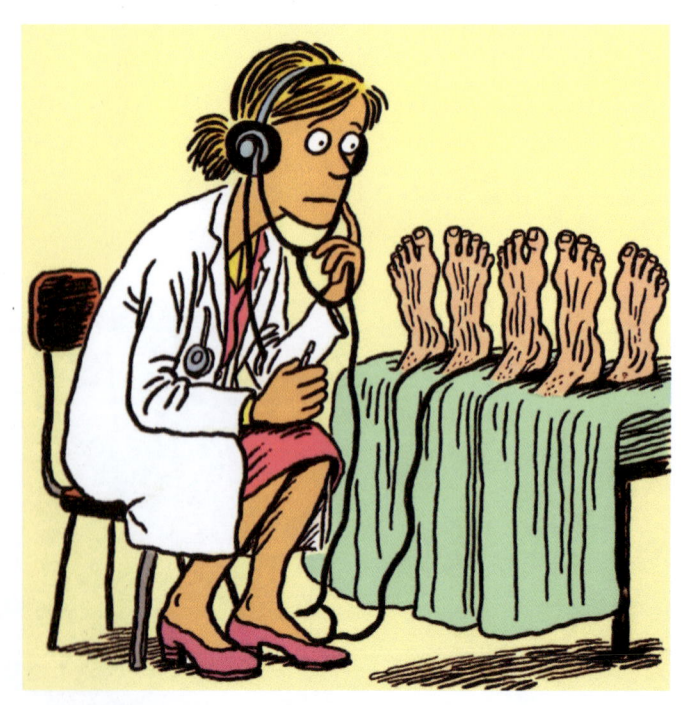

What is a foot doctor's favorite thing to listen to?

Podcasts.

What did the podiatrist call
his patient after their flat foot was fixed?

Archie.

Why did the podiatrist lose their job when they moved to Europe?

There are no feet – everything is metric!

Did you hear about the police who tried to get the axon to commit a crime?

It was nerve entrapment.

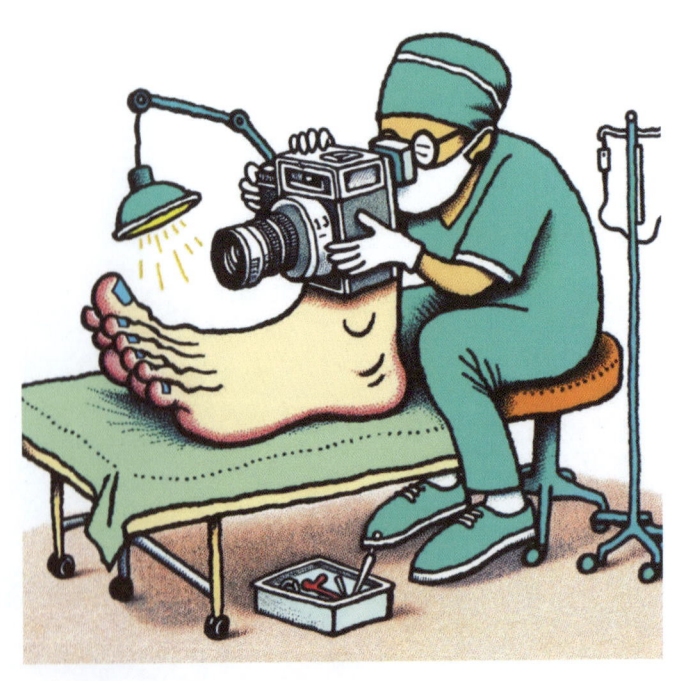

Why did the podiatrist always videotape her surgeries?

She wanted to get some great footage.

How do you know a leg is lying?

It has a fib-ula.

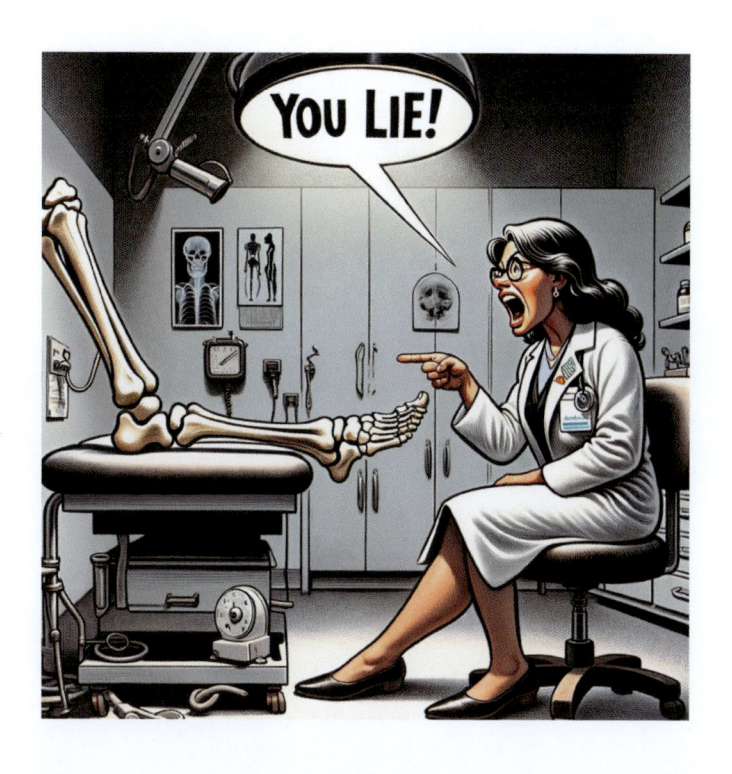

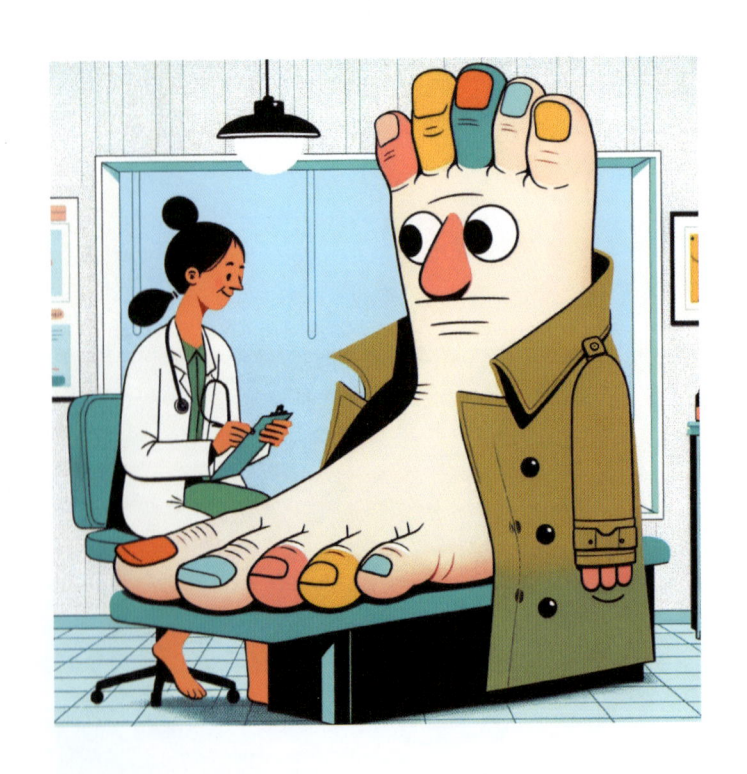

Why don't trench coats
go any lower than the ankles?

Any further and you'd have trench foot.

Did you hear about the patient who hurt his heel while licking his keyboard?

He had a tongue-type calcaneus fracture.

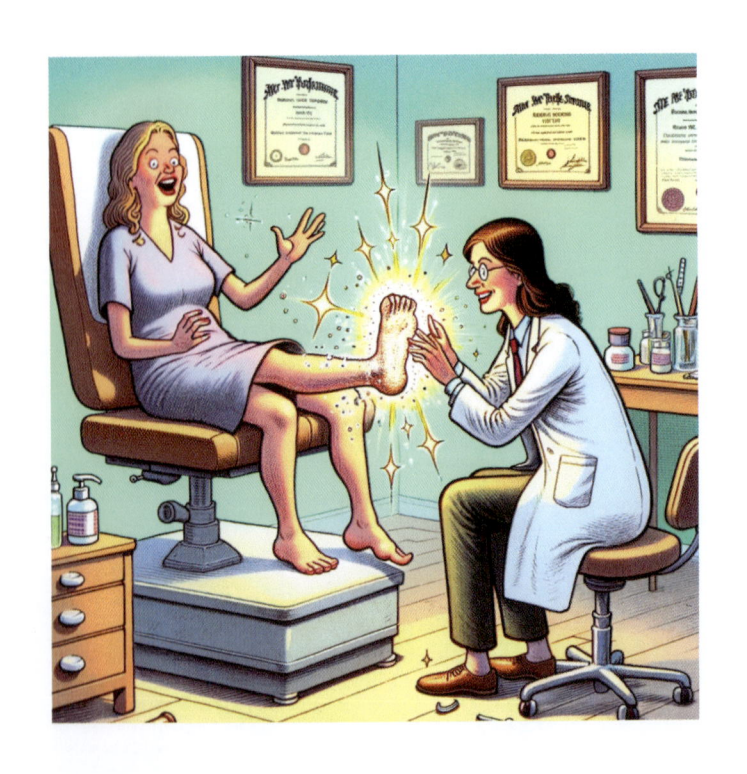

If you have a problem with the back of your foot, why should you see a podiatrist?

Because they're heel-ors.

Who's a podiatrist's favorite pop star?

Talar Swift.

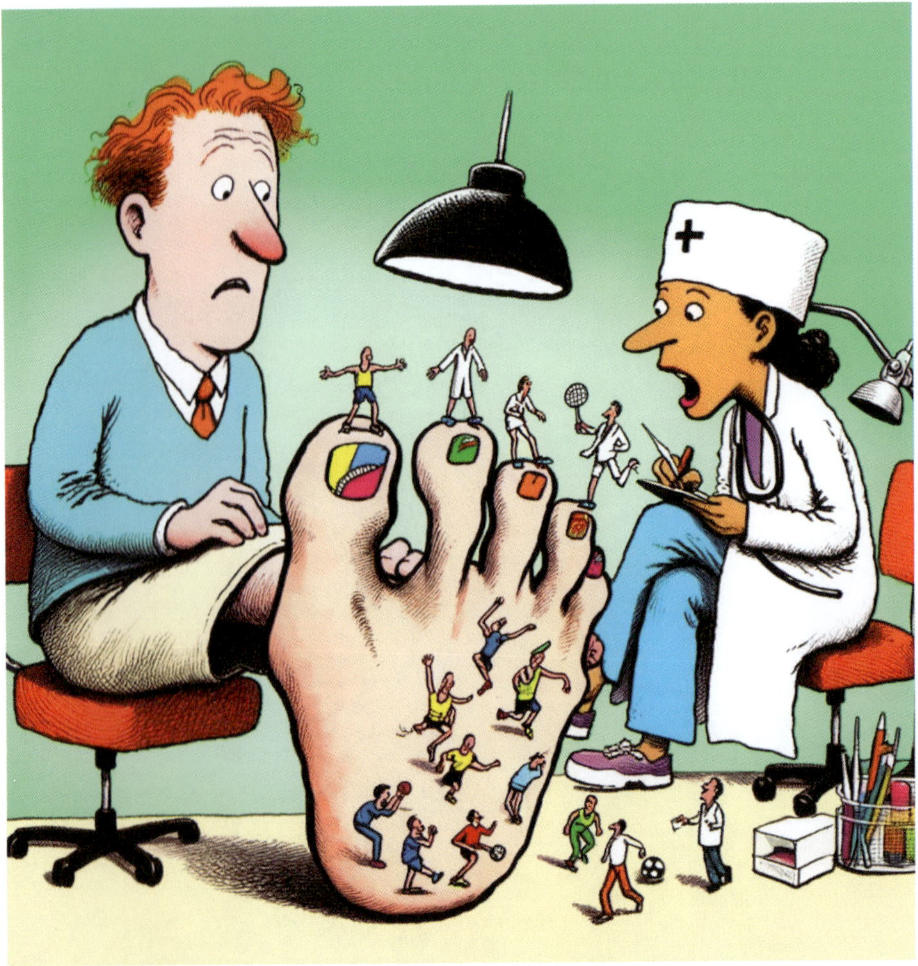

A patient goes to a podiatrist and says,

"You have to help me. I have all these tiny basketball and baseball players on my toes."

The podiatrist says,

"Sounds like you have athlete's foot."

Did you hear about the podiatrist
who treated 500 patients in a day?

What a feet!

How do podiatrists count?

One, toe, three...

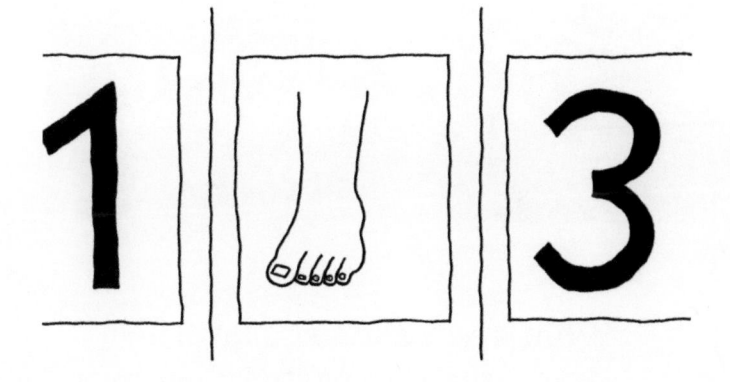

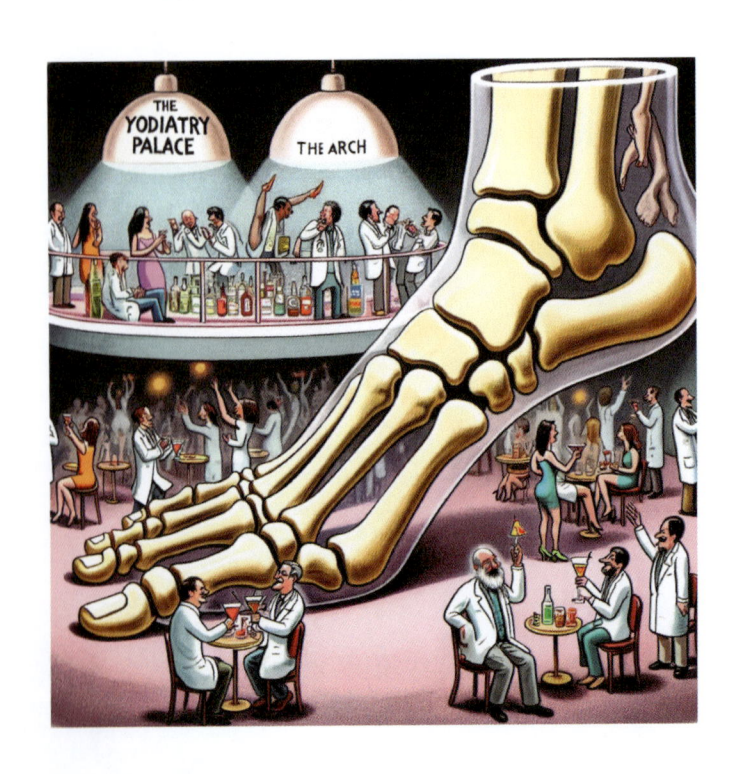

What's a podiatrist's favorite place to party?

Club foot.

What does a podiatrist like on her bagel?

Sesamoid seeds.

How is a podiatrist like a pastor?

She'll save your sole.

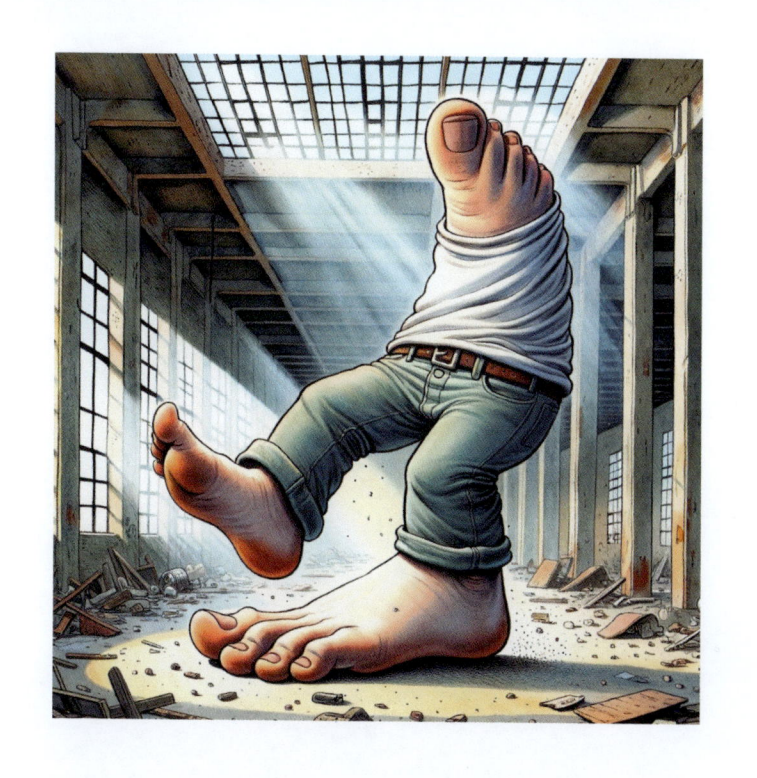

What's a podiatrist's favorite movie?

Footloose.

Why did the podiatrist keep a saddle in her office?

In case a patient had equinus.

What is a podiatrist's favorite sport?

Football.

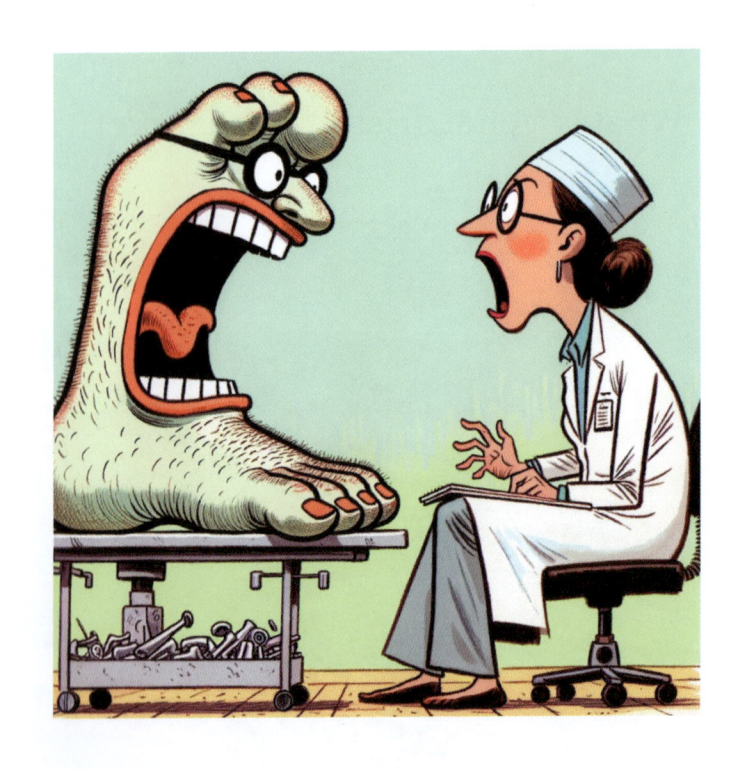

Why did the podiatrist refuse to treat the rude foot?

He was quite callus.

Why should you go to a podiatrist to be impressed?

They'll knock your socks off.

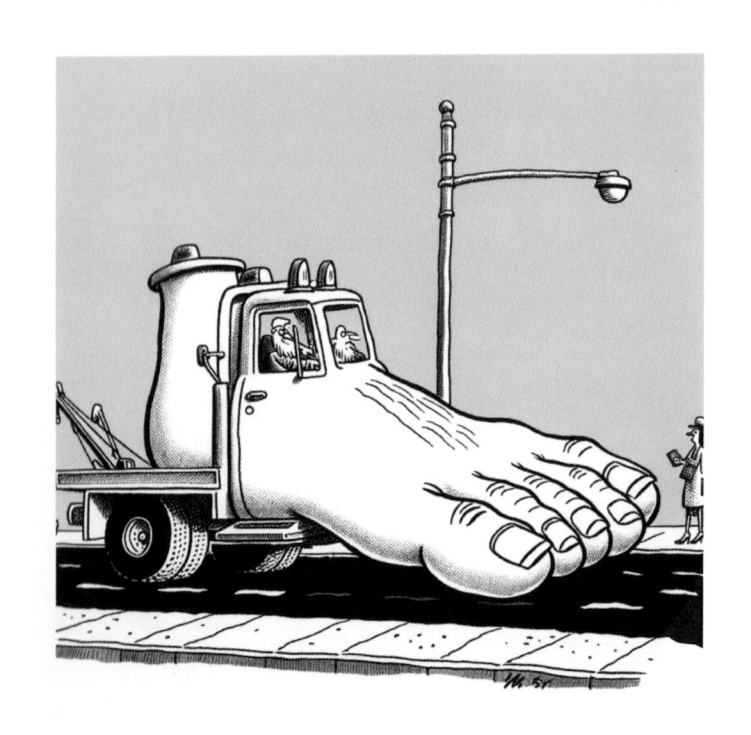

What's a podiatrist's favorite type of vehicle?

Toe truck.

Did you hear about the podiatrist who successfully performed an avulsion?

They nailed it.

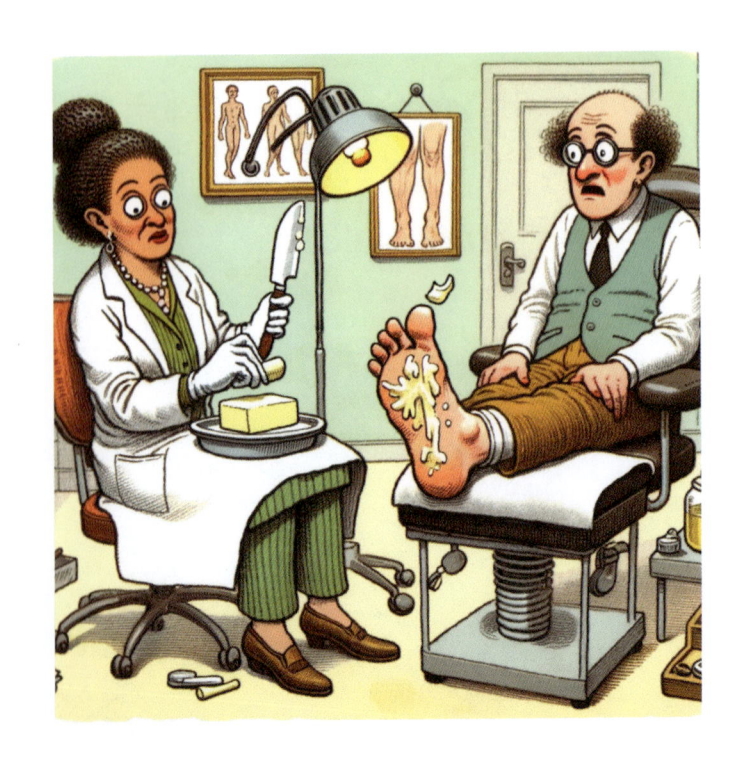

How does a podiatrist use
butter to treat patients?

They put it on corns.

How can you tell when you get
to a podiatrist's house?

Look at the gait.

Sasquatch tells his podiatrist,

"Doc, my right shoe feels tighter than my left. What do I have?"

The podiatrist replies,

"Bigfoot."

53

Printed in Dunstable, United Kingdom